MW01611440

From Idea
to
Implementation

NIURKA CASTANEDA

Published by

Niurka Castaneda

Copyright © 2021 Niurka Castaneda

All rights reserved. Except as permitted under the United States Copyright Act of 1976, no part of this publication in any format, photographic, mechanic, electronic, in the forms of photographic recording or physical, may it be transmitted, reproduced or distributed in any form or by any means, stored or otherwise copied in a database or retrieval system for public and private use other than for "fair use" as brief quotations in articles and review without prior written permission the publisher.

For information about special discounts for bulk purchases, please contact AMOR umbrella at bulk@amorumbrella.com

Softcover ISBN: 978-1-7364815-2-3
Ebook ISBN: 978-1-7364815-5-4
Hardcover ISBN: 979-8-9855579-7-8
Library of Congress Control Number: 2022904641

The information provided in this book is for informational purposes only and is not intended to be a source of advice or credit analysis with respect to the material presented. The information and/or documents contained in this book do not constitute legal or financial advice and should never be used without first consulting with a financial or legal professional to determine what may be best for your individual needs.

Cover Design: Alejandro Castaneda
Interior: Niurka Castaneda

Printed by Ventures C & A LLC in the United States of America
1st Edition 1 MAR 2022
AMOR umbrella
Miami, FL 33197
www.amorumbrella.com

Dedication & Acknowledgement

For my family,
for each and every person who has helped me believe in myself,
in a mission greater than myself, in the great potential each of
us has and to the most authentic, creative, bravest people I
know: The Entrepreneurs of the World.

PROLOGUE

Whether you are exploring a new endeavor or idea, **From Idea to Implementation**© will guide you in how to better organize and launch them to make them tangible…It will give you the steps for developing, framing, testing, and getting them to market quickly.

Hey there!

This guide will give you insight into what it takes to launch your new ideas.

- Don't limit yourself or your ideas. Learn to **DREAM BIG** and **STEP OUT OF THE BOX.**

- Learn to **TRUST YOURSELF** and take it **ONE STEP AT A TIME.**

- **VALIDATE & PRIORITIZE** your ideas.

- The key is to just **START**, to take imperfect **ACTION** but to start **Lean and Mean** and to always remember: "**Cash is King**".

Learn to be conservative with your funds from the beginning, have at least a fundamental knowledge of what is needed before you hire out, and learn your business numbers.

FOCUS ON THE BASICS

Launching a business idea is pretty simple. . . but it is not necessarily an easy endeavor. Don't get distracted by too many ideas or by trying to make all of them happen at the same time. Take the time to plan, to organize and to take imperfect action.

Ideas to Implementation Checklist	PG	N/A	Not Done	Done
1 Ideas	10			
2 Protect Your Ideas	15			
3 Creativity	21			
4 Problem Solving	24			
5 Brainstorming	28			
6 Other Techniques to Generate Ideas	32			
7 Organize Your Ideas	34			
8 Problem Solving	38			
9 Identify Your Customer	42			
10 Creating Your Minimum Value Product	47			
11 Time To Launch	49			

Where are the ideas?

Ideas are everywhere...

Inspiration, that Eureka or creative moment can strike at any time, sometimes in the most inconvenient places.

Creativity can come from new experiences, from things that break, out of challenges, from the difficult times in life, and/or from the things we learn.

When we take actions with these ideas is when we transform them into something we can see, hear, or experience.

"If you can dream it, you can do it" —Walt Disney

Some ideas can take shape in a moment or slowly become a piece of art.

Why? Some people are quick to start, but they are slow to finish. They are often called procrastinators.

Are you one?

It is not a bad thing to be a procrastinator. Procrastination is a trait that may actually help boost his or her creativity, because by taking the longer road, they often diverge and learn new things along the way, enriching their perspective that they can later apply to their ideas.

Did you know that Leonardo da Vinci worked for 16 years to create the Mona Lisa? He used to procrastinate and that often led him to feel like a failure according to his journal. He took many learning detours that ultimately taught him how to model light and made him into a much better painter.

Did you know that Martin Luther King, Jr. stayed awake until 3 a.m. the night before the biggest speech of his life? Even later while sitting in the audience, waiting on his turn, he was still preparing, rewriting and doing last minute tweaks to the script. Did you know that the 4 words that made it history, "I have a dream..." were not in the original script? He had left himself open to inspiration and improvisation.

On the other hand, procrastinators, according to David Rosenbaum, a professor of psychology at the University of California, Riverside, who coined the name, tend to start very early, even months earlier and start getting ready by pre-planning or by creating a to-do list. They tend not to be as creative and are more rational thinkers. It is not a bad thing to be because it is very satisfying to check things off, but it can also dampen their creativity.

Are you a **procrastinator**?

The best course of action is to plan your creativity days by not doing any pre-planning at all or anything that can be considered mechanical to slow you down and open yourself to inspiration by generating as many ideas as possible. It is a simple process called brainstorming that can be very useful and that we will be exploring in this guide.

DO YOU DARE TO TRY?

Remember:
"Creativity is intelligence having fun "
—Albert Einstein

Disclosure: *It is recommended that you seek the advice of a CPA for taxes purposes and the advice of an attorney for legal purposes.*

1.   IDEAS

All businesses start with an idea. Startups are born because there is a problem that needs a solution.

Those solutions or ideas can be simple or revolutionary, and inspiration can strike you from all sorts of sources. Your own personal struggles or necessities, everyday puzzles, driving passions, the subconscious mind, and opportunities that you experience.

And as a new entrepreneur, you will have many ideas that can contribute to your success. However, it is the actions that you take with them that make all the difference.

Some ideas might be better than others, but you will never know their true potential until you dare to make them happen. It is all about making them tangible and figuring out how to apply them to make the idea or solution **spreadable and profitable**.

You will be surprised to learn that the value of an idea, good or bad, is $0.00. If you DO NOT **EXECUTE** it and **TAKE ACTION**, it will still be worth $0.0. Execution of your ideas is primordial, not to keep waiting until everything is perfect. Good or bad ideas if executed right, can generate money, and remember, they do not exclusively belong to you.

How many times have you thought about something, but because you didn't have the time, the money or the resources, decided not to pursue them and later you saw them sitting on the store shelf because somebody else thought of it too, and they **TOOK ACTION** and took it to market.

"Life is a daring adventure or nothing at all "—Helen Keller

History has proven it does not necessarily have to be a good or wise idea in order to be successful. There are people that made money with strange, unusual, and sometimes even pointless inventions that started with just an idea.

Have you ever heard the story of the pet rock?

The Pet Rock, was a fad that was first introduced at "The Annual San Francisco Gift Show" by marketing genius and creator Gary Dahl.

He turned into an instant millionaire. with this silly, crazy, incredible and genius... idea. Did you know that they made a whopping 15M in just 6 month....?

What....? Yes, you heard right, 15M dollars in just 6 month

How is that possible?

It all started with a joke in a bar. The conversation among friends had turned to the cost of pets, how they can be quite destructive at times and the time involved. Gary Dahl replied that he didn't have to wonder about any of these things because he had a pet rock. Everyone laughed. It was a joke, but a joke made him think that he should try to see how far he could go. He began to develop his idea and he created an instruction manual on how to train this pet, and he packaged it inside a cardboard box with breathing holes and an excelsior bed for the stony pet.

He sourced the smooth stones from Rosarito, Mexico, and cost him 1 cent. He was able to sell them to retail stores for $2 each in bulk and individually to the consumer for $3.95.

Let's it break it down

They sold for $3.95, and had a profit of $3 per sale.

Each rock cost the inventor 0.1 cents

He sold them for $2.00 to retailers.

At one time he was shipping 10k pet rocks a day. He could barely keep up with the demand.

By now you might be scratching your head and asking yourself:

Were they made of gold? No, they were simple rocks that got marketed as "hassle free" companions.

What was included?

They included a hay bed in a cardboard box with breathing holes as a pet carrier, a pet training and instruction manual on how to deal with this new housemate.

Despite the fad being over just 6 month later it does show you what the perceived value of an IDEA is and the positive outcomes that can come out of it and taught us many valuable lessons.

It was conceived in 1975 at a time when people needed a good laugh during the Vietnam War. Ghal sold not just a stone but an experience. The perceived value and price was seen as reasonable, because it solved a problem for the mother who could not afford a pet for her children but could buy a rock for $3.95, or for people who did not want to suffer the death or destruction that a pet can bring and did not need extra care.

Do you still think his idea was too silly?
Do you remember what Roosevelt once said?
> "It is hard to fail, but it is worse never to have tried to succeed."—Theodore Roosevelt

Sometimes ideas might not be silly at all, but they fail because it just was not the right time to implement them.

> Did you know that no one bought **sliced bread** (invented by Otto Rohwedder) 15 years after it was available? It wasn't until Wonder came along and marketed the idea to the masses that it became a success. By every normal standard, it could be considered a total failure.

It is best to be flexible and be willing to always improve on the original idea.
Be Prepared to Shift Gears
Keep on tweaking your ideas.

That is why it is important to take the time to analyze your ideas or solutions and determine the problem that they are solving and who is willing to pay for them.

Do you know that one out of every 13 children have food

FROM IDEA TO IMPLEMENTATION

allergies?

Iris Shamus's son is one of them. He's seriously allergic to peanuts. In order to make sure that his teachers and caretakers always remembered his son's allergies, she developed the **AllerMates**, a cute bracelet that depicts which allergy the child has. It is now sold in 7,000 locations across the United States.

Do your children like to receive mail from Santa?

SantaMail, started by Byron Reese, has sent over 200,000 letters since 2001 (at $10 each) to solve that problem.

Do you want to do math?

200,000 x $10.00 = ?

2. PROTECTING YOUR IDEAS

A good exercise to practice to keep all your ideas safe is to start a **"Business Ideas Journal"** while you are brainstorming business ideas that will help you clarify and visualize your thoughts and ideas.

You can maintain a record for each idea and decide which has a better possibility of making it to market later. Do not discard the other ones. You might be able to implement them later.

Remember that a good business idea does not just have to be profitable; it has to fit your personality, your target market, and your location. If you want to succeed and stay for the long haul, you should pick something that you are passionate about, not just something that would make you money.

> *"Ideas Are Abundant; Drive Isn't ... "*
> — Samer Kurdi, Chairman of the Global Board, Entrepreneurs' Organization (Hartman, 2022)

Do not be afraid of thinking BIG.

The bigger or more impossible your ideas seem, the better. When you allow yourself to dream big, the more open to possibilities and the more resourceful you become to make them happen. Aim to make the world a better place with your ideas, learn from your failures, and pivot quickly when needed be.

Don't forget to protect your ideas.

An important step to consider in order to protect your valuable ideas is to consider taking legal measures like consulting with a lawyer and/or consider filing for a trademark, copyright, trade dress unfair competition laws, trade secrets or patent. Not all options would be applicable at the same time.

Depending on the nature of your ideas you should consider what legal measure is the most appropriate. Your name, your intellectual property, your products, your business or domain will become part of your brand and are things that you must consider protecting in order to gain legal protection and offer you the right to license them later to a third party.

For example Disney, provides licenses to toymakers and distributors that defines how they may manufacture & distribute Disney merchandise.

Things to consider:
How many people are involved in your idea?
How much time and money would you have to invest?
How valuable is your idea?
Is it easy to replicate?

The kind of approach that you should consider would change depending upon whether your ideas have intellectual original value, whether it is a new invention, or if it is a new design, a mark, a domain, etc. It can get confusing. It is advisable to consult with an attorney.

LEGAL MEASURES TO PROTECT YOUR IDEAS

1. Patent

The symbol that is used to represent a Patent is: ®.
It is a right approved and granted by the U.S government that would prevent others from selling, making or distributing your invention. It is a process that can take up to 2 years. Your rights would not begin until the patent is granted.

2. Trademark

The symbol that is used to represent a Trademark is: ™.

It can apply to a word, mark or symbol that would make your product, service or company recognizable. In the US a trademark is filed with the USPTO. To further complicate matters, US trademarks only protect you in the US, not internationally. While considering using your ideas overseas, a new trademark protection must be filed in that particular country. There are several examples of classes listed below. Not all classes would apply, it would depend on what kind (physical, digital or intellectual) of idea or product you have. It can get confusing, so seeking legal advice is recommended.

For example, these are some of the 45 international classes to consider. The trademark application must be specific on what items include, you would have to provide a specimen (a photo) as proof of use and it must fit into one of the available international classes:

- Class 9 Downloadable book
- Class 10 Face mask
- Class 14 Jewelry
- Class 16 Books and Educational Products, Printing books
- Class 18 Umbrella and carrying cases, travel bags, bookbag, backpack, scratch bags
- Class 25: Clothing and apparel, accessories
- Class 28 Toys teddy bears, surfboards
- Class 35 Online retail store services like clothing, apparel, mugs, cups, umbrellas, covers for mobile devices, and accessories
- Class 38 Video streaming, visual vision
- Class 41 Production

Be warned that once a trademark class protection has been granted, the legal protection that it provides would only last for

5 years and then you would have to file for renewal. Also if you stop using the mark in a specific class for more than 3 years it would be considered an abandoned mark.

3. Copyright

According to the current law, the author of the creative work owns the copyright of the work once it is made tangible by painting it, making it, writing it or typing it in your computer unless a legal contractual agreement has been set in place by an individual, publishing company, a business, etc. A copyright filed in the US would only protect your work in those countries that the US has a copyright relationship with.

The symbol that is used to represent a Copyright is: ©. Getting official proof that you own the work is easy to obtain by filing directly with eCO Online System, (3 to 4 months) or sending paperwork by regular mail (5 to 8 months) to obtain copyright approval.

Ex: Niurka Castaneda (c) 2020. All rights reserved.

4. Trade Dress Unfair Competition laws

In order for your idea to fall under the trade dress category it must be distinctive enough in order to stop competition from using it.

5. Trade Secrets

The way to protect trade secrets is by putting security measures in place to protect those secrets like:
- Limiting access to only those who need to know
- Use proper labeling
- Secure your computers and trade secret documents
- Monitoring who has access

6. Registration

Consider registration of a business, a product or a domain to protect it.

7. Confidential Agreement

Depending if you have to contract the services of another person or company and there is a need for confidentiality, you should consider having a confidentiality agreement prepared by an attorney that makes them legally liable for any breach of confidentiality.

Confidentiality agreements are also name:
- A non-disclosure agreement (NDA)
- Confidentiality disclosure agreement (CDA)
- Proprietary Information Agreement (PIA)
- Secrecy Agreement (SA)

Beware: Do not use a generic form downloaded from the internet, always make sure it fits the situation and consult with an attorney.

8. Work for Hire agreement

When contracting a third party, enforcing a work for hire agreement temporarily will assure that you actually own the work that you are commissioning because even if you are paying for it, the transfer of ownership of intellectual property is not automatic. It will help to define the scope of the work and what are the responsibilities of each party. It should include and clearly define:

- A timeline for the project
- Terms of payment
- A detailed work schedule
- Project milestones

9. Watermark

It is a mark or text of a lighter shade that appears in a picture of a document used to protect intellectual assets and clearly state ownership. It is traditionally used by artists, or photographers to protect their work, but it also can be used in a word document using the word DRAFT in order to avoid theft or unauthorized use of the work.

3. CREATIVITY

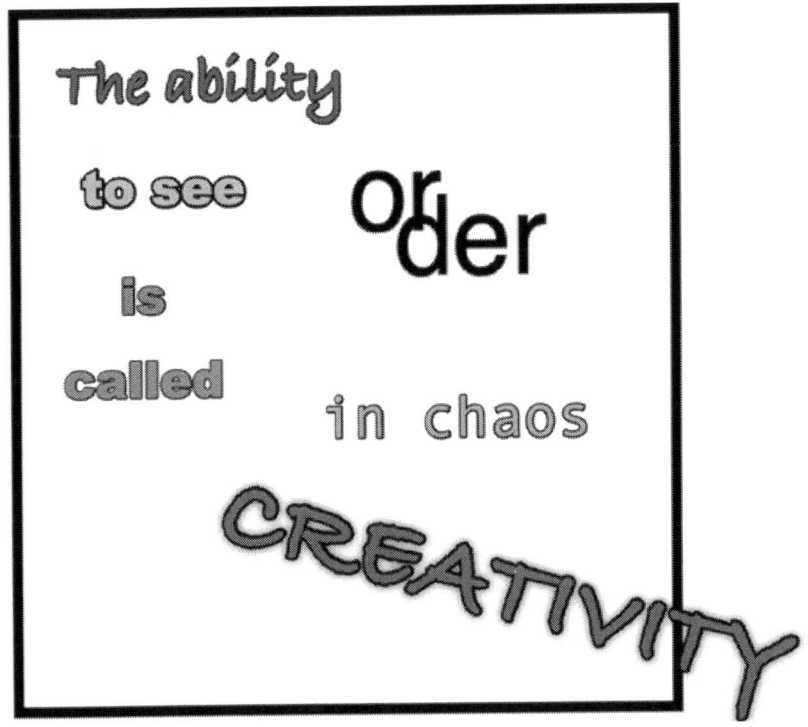

Creativity is not limited to artists, it can be practiced by everyone. It is the process of developing your ideas in both a novel and practical way.

Don't be afraid to step out of the traditional box way of thinking. Allow yourself to be bold and allow your ideas to flow... the more you do, the more ideas you will have... Remember that creativity is the foundation of innovation.

Tom Kelley explains in his book The Ten Faces of Innovation.

> *"Innovation is ultimately a team sport. Get all the roles performing at the top of their game, and you'll generate a positive force for innovation."*(Kelley & Littman, 2008)

When you are starting up, you really don't know where you are going to go...

Don't believe me?

Did you know about a company called Google?

They started with the idea that they wanted to be a nonprofit to help find information until they realized their business had infinite applications.

Would you believe that YouTube started as a gaming dating site?

Believe it or not, it is true, and look at them now.

When you have an idea, one of the things you need to figure out is who are the player(s) that will help you transform that idea into a tangible solution that can spread like wildfire.

> *"You don't want curious people; you want committed people because when they get bored, they are gone. Your business is all about people"*—Steven Hoffman

Avoid hiring family, unless it is a family business, even though from a tax perspective it can be good, but you want people that you can fire if they don't work out.

A resource that you can use for insight in applying innovation is the Ten Faces of Innovation book by Tom Kelley, a Partner at IDEO, where he groups them into 3 categories.

Remember to have fun with your ideas because when you get stressed your chances of failure go up.

If you would like to dive in deeper on the concept of creative problem solving, some additional resources that we recommend for you to explore are:

Video: Elizabeth Wimer - Creative Problem Solving

Creative Thinking: How to Increase the Dots to Connect

Navi Radjou: Creative problem-solving in the face of

extreme limits

Where good ideas come from | Steven Johnson

The art of innovation | Guy Kawasaki | TEDxBerkeley

4. PROBLEM SOLVING

Start by doing this exercise:

Grab a piece of paper and draw 9 dots.

O   O   O

O   O   O

O   O   O

Now proceed to connect the 9 dots without raising your pen or crossing over the lines in the following one minute.

Once you are done connecting the dots you might realize that you had a difficult time connecting all 9 dots or you might have tried to form a square.

Your picture might look like some variation of the following drawing:

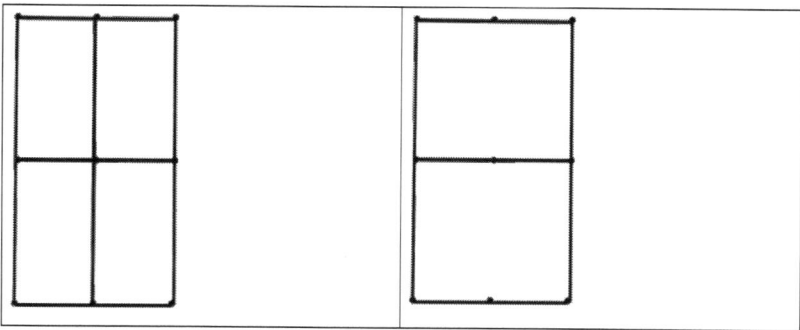

However, if you re-read the instructions again it is not mentioned anywhere that you need to form a square or rectangle shape. You could have connected the dots in several different ways without having to create a rectangle or square box.

This exercise illustrates how most of us are subconsciously stuck in the traditional way of thinking, but in order to come up with creative solutions, you would need to literally *step out of the box and be open to creative solutions.*

Are you ready to use some creative thinking?

Creative thinking is valued by business and entrepreneurs alike because it is a process that allows you to be innovative and progressive. It allows for growth.

You can combine unrelated ideas, products, people, materials, features or services to create something new. It is an effective way to generate new ideas, solutions or answers to problems.

Ask yourself:

What can I combine or merge together to build synergy or achieve a particular result?

Let's explore several techniques that stimulate creative thinking. Apply each method individually or mix them up to get unstuck.

5.   BRAINSTORMING

Brainstorming is a revolutionary but simple technique used in creative thinking that was developed by Alex Osborn in 1941 that stimulates new ideas and assists you to fight conventional business ways inhibiting new ideas.

The development of this technique changed the world and the way we think. It is a proven technique that since its introduction has spread across the world as an effective way to come up with ideas and solutions. Since its inception, brainstorming has spread like wildfire and it is being used every day around the world and can help you get unstuck.

You can read more about this original approach in Alex Osborn's book "Applied Imagination".

How many times have you brainstormed to find the solution to a problem?

Probably more than once.

Brainstorming is a crucial part of the writing and/ or creative process. It is an activity that can be practiced in groups or individually. While practicing brainstorming, it is good to emphasize creativity and avoid naysaying.

Do you know that brainstorming encourages generating silly ideas?

Alex Osborn found that they could spark off very useful ideas because they changed the way people thought.

Since its introduction, brainstorming has been used to develop:

- Advertising campaigns
- Research and Development procedures
- Research techniques
- Patents
- Written documents, books and articles

- Services
- Marketing strategy and methods
- Physical products
- Management methods
- Processes
- Engineering components
- Company structure and policy
- Government policies
- Consumer research
- Investment decisions
- New industries

And the list continues...

Avoid unproductive brainstorming sessions and increase your rate of success by applying the IDEO U's general rules:

> Defer judgment, Encourage wild ideas, Build on the ideas of others, Stay focused on the topic, One conversation at a time, Be visual and Go for quantity. (IDEO U)

Follow the six-step method

1. Prepare by setting aside time for it.
    A. Schedule it.
    B. Avoid distractions.
    C. Set the mood to help you think.
    D. Write it down.

2. Write down your main or focus point to help you snap back to the main point if you get distracted.

3. Write down all your ideas, even if they are obvious.
    A. Make room for new ideas.
    B. Focus on quantity not quality.
    C. There are no bad ideas in brainstorming.

4.   Look for patterns.
              A.   Look for similarities.
              B.   Connect the dots.

5. Analyze all your ideas for gaps or holes.

              A.   List all the missing areas or plots.
              B.   Use it as a checklist to check your progress.

6. Address the missing gaps by generating new ideas. Some suggested techniques that you can use for this section:

              A.   Word association technique allows you to recall and write down new words.

              - For example: the word "ice" would make you think of "cold", "cold" would make you think of "winter", "winter" would make you think of "coat"…

              B.   Ask questions.

              - For example: What is she thinking? What is she feeling? What is the supporting evidence?

              C.   Ask "What if…" scenarios to your questions.

              - For example: what if she was younger?

Supplies you would need to start brainstorming

POST-IT(™) notes, have at least three different colors

Markers

A wall or flat surface

If you prefer to use a visual app for your brainstorming session, you can try BoardThing or Trello.

Are you ready to brainstorm?

6. OTHER TECHNIQUES TO GENERATE IDEAS

There are many other tools and resources like the ones we've discussed previously that can assist you in the process of creativity and to organize your ideas.

However, the key thing is to pick 2 or 3 that work for you and start practicing with them. The more you allow yourself to be creative and don't put restrictions on your imagination, the easier it is to awaken your creativity.

Other techniques that you can explore are listed below.

Random Word Technique

This technique is very simple. You use a random word as a prompt to generate word association and generate ideas.

For example:

Word: Hot

New idea: shade

Bridging idea: find or create a spot that you can shade yourself from the hot weather

Random Picture Technique

This technique is similar to the random word, but instead of using a word, you use a picture to ideate a solution to a problem that you can associate with that picture.

Random Website Technique

This technique is one where you analyze other websites to gather inspiration to apply to your own idea.

Search and Reapply Technique

This is where you look at other competitors in your field or other industries to see what solution they are offering. What similar problems have been solved? What areas of expertise have been applied? What industry? What solutions can be reapplied to your own idea?

Wishful Thinking Technique

Most of us are familiar with this technique where we imagine our ideal solution or situation. What would you do if money were not an objection? What would you do if there were no limits? Once you have come up with your ideal solution or situation, then you start ideating how you can make it happen.

Escape Technique

With this technique there are no limitations to your imagination. You can propose the wackiest, most outrageous, the wildest or silliest ideas. They do not have to be sensible, practical, or possible.

7. ORGANIZE YOUR IDEAS

Once you open your mind to the possibilities and start brainstorming potential solutions to a problem or analyzing a specific situation, you might end up having several ideas coming at you and that can make it hard to sort through them. All of that might end up making you feel overwhelmed or indecisive as to what is the best action to take and upon which idea to act first.

Remember that when you practice brainstorming by yourself or with a team, you do not want to censor your ideas in any way or shape, and you want to allow for as many ideas as possible. That is part of the process!!!

Write them all down on a sticky note, a flip chart, a tablet, or a spreadsheet while the inspiration strikes.

Make it a habit to review the ideas when you need to revisit inspiration or to gradually roll them out once the timing is right. It is also a great way to keep the spirit of innovation alive for your business.

One handy tool that you can use to help you organize your ideas is the KJ Method known by many other names like the affinity diagram, mapping, sorting, snowballing or even as card sorting. This type of diagram will allow you to draw out and identify the common themes from all of your ideas.

1. Organize your ideas to see if they can be stacked, chunked, or grouped together to see if they have a similarity or are connected in any way.

2. If any of the ideas cannot be grouped or stacked together, keep them separate as a standalone.

3. If they can fit into more than one column, make a duplicate card.

4. Limit the themes to 5 to 9 themes.

What are the connections between all your ideas or information?

It will also allow you to brainstorm root causes and solutions to a problem.

RANDOM IDEAS   **AFFINITY DIAGRAM**

Theme 1   Theme 1   Theme 1

To practice you can use this exercise:

1. Create an Affinity Map to identify new ways to think about the problem first for 10 minutes. At this stage, do not think about solutions, just the problem.

    To accomplish this, you can use regular paper sticky notes on a white board or if working remotely, you can use an app like:

    > Miro

    > Jamboard by Google

    > Independently, each team member should select a unique note color and post their ideas.

    > Write one potential problem for each sticky note only.

After the 10 minutes of brainstorming for ideas has passed, share with the rest of your group looking for similar insights.

Create clusters of similar insights.

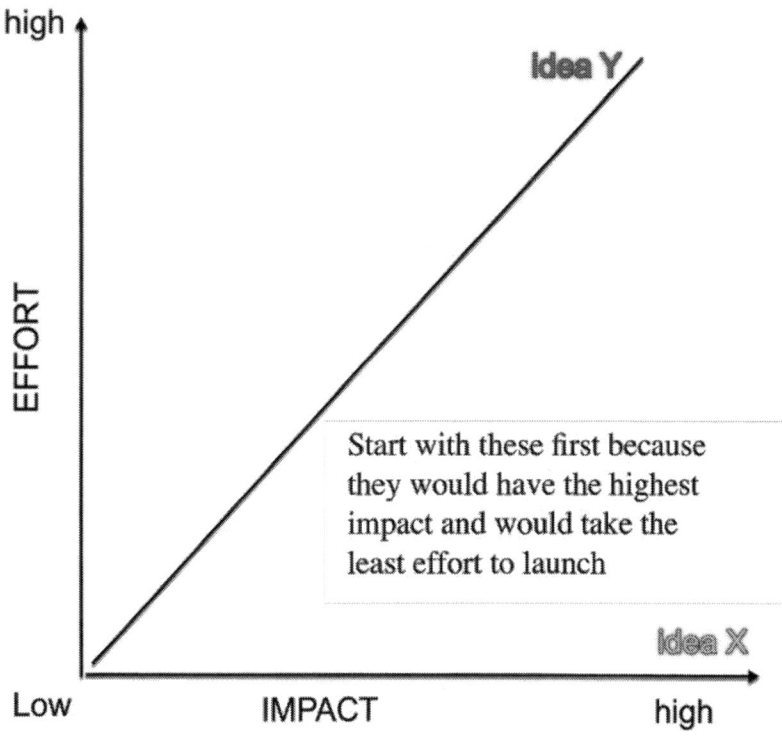

At the end of your brainstorming section, gather all your ideas and analyze them. Some of them might take longer to develop or might be infeasible because of a key missing element. A way to sort and prioritize them is by creating a scale to determine the effort and impact that it would take to make that idea happen.

It is important to define the impact that your idea would have whether your idea is a product, a service, a feature of a product, or a solution to a problem for the end user that would benefit from it.**8. PROBLEM SOLVING**

There are different methods that can help you reach creative problem-solving.

A favorite method that starts by first knowing what the problem that's being solved is called Design Thinking.

What is it?

According to Tim Brown, Executive Chair of IDEO :

"Design Thinking is a human centered-approach to innovation that draws from the designer toolkit to integrate the need of people, the possibilities of technology and the requirement for business success " (IDEO U)

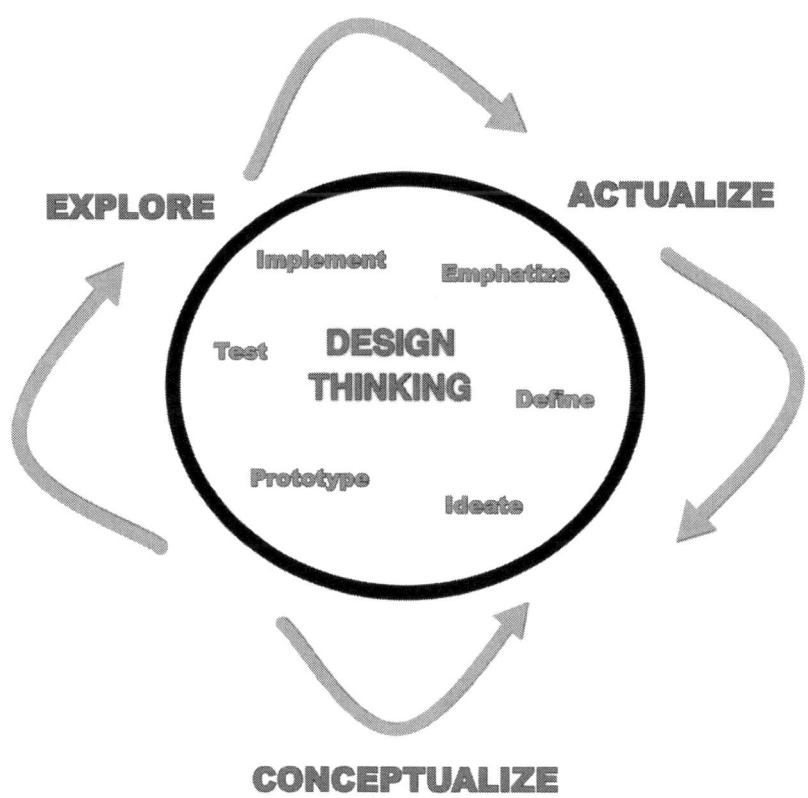

Should you apply this method when generating ideas?

Design Thinking is more than a way to generate innovative ideas, it is a mindset that starts with people.

- It can be used for any product and is human centered.
- It is an inclusive process that welcomes any idea and solution.
- It will help frame and reframe the problem.
- It applies convergent and divergent thinking.
- It will allow you to test and implement your ideas to see if they work.

It is used by big corporations like Apple, Nordstrom, Starbucks, IBM, Bank of America, IDEO U, Nike and Oral B among others that decided to integrate this method in order to develop their products and be able to empathize with their customers.

The best way to **APPLY IT** is by **DOING IT** and **EXPERIENCING IT**.

Make sure every single voice is heard, that means the introverts and extroverts, in order to capture all ideas. We can do this by using sticky **POST IT** ™ notes. The reason why we want to use **POST IT** ™ notes as opposed to a big blank paper is because it will make it less intimidating.

Be warned!!!

It is not supposed to be a neat process but a messy process that helps you generate and capture all your ideas.

There are several resources where you can generate ideas using this problem solving method.

A good website to gather additional information in this topic is:

Design Minded

Use the **HOW** approach to find all the possible solutions in a collaborative way by asking yourself and your team:

How might we solve this problem?

> Think about all the possible solutions; however, you don't want to jump into the solution right away but actually try to understand the problem you are solving.

Are you collaborating with a team **for** the Ideation Stage?

A great site to check is designminded.me/jmi to find several exercises activities that you can practice with a team of four to six people.

Design Thinking has 3 phases:

- Inspiration
- Ideation
- Implementation

> Start by identifying your stakeholders (the people, groups or individuals who can have an impact or will be impacted by your idea or product).

> Use a tool like Mind Tool or just a simple piece of paper to map your stakeholders:

> Mind Tool

> Remember that while applying a method like Design Thinking you want to collect all possible solutions and decide which ones are best to adopt.

The steps of applying Design Thinking are.

1.   Start at the end

> A.   MAP
> B.   Ask the experts
> C.   Target

2. **Remix & Improve**
   A. Sketch
   B. Refine
   C. Improve
3. **Decide**
   A. Rumble
   B. Storyboard

Once you have gone through the 3 steps you should proceed to create a prototype in order to test your ideas.

9. IDENTIFY YOUR CUSTOMER

Who would benefit from your ideas?

In other words, to whom are you going to market your ideas?

Understanding who your potential customer is would allow you to be able to communicate effectively to that person.

What if you don't have any customers?

Create a marketing persona (also called an emphatic map) that would be a representation of your ideal customer.

Put yourself in their shoes to learn about the **Demographic** and **Psychographic** characteristics of your prospect.

Demographics are the statistical data gathered from a particular population like your potential customer's age, income, gender, etc..

Psychographics refers to your potential customer's attitudes, goals and other psychological criteria.

You need to understand what motivates them, their attitudes, their behaviors and the desired outcome for your customers. Depending on your ideas and business applications, you might need more than one persona.

Why would you need to create a buyer persona?

Creating a buyer persona would not only allow you to

36

understand your customer (future and present) better, but it would help you improve your marketing and communication processes.

Remember to avoid faulty assumptions by doing quantitative and qualitative research.

- Talk to actual people and get feedback on your ideas
- Conduct surveys

An example of a survey that worked was one conducted by Seventeen Magazine. They created their persona back in 1950 based on data they collected from a survey they did during the mid 1940s targeting teenage girls and their mothers. They named this persona Teena.

The persona was as insecure as the teenagers that were reading the magazine. Since they launched in 1950, their persona has undergone several changes, but they reflected their persona in their magazine by capitalizing and focusing their content on your girls' insecurities.

Use a template like the one offered by HubSpot to guide you through the process of creating your marketing persona.

Another method that you can use after building your marketing persona is called Journey Mapping where you map all the touch points where your present and future customers would come in contact with your ideas. This method can also be applied to projects, products or even your own brand.

Ask questions like:

1. Who are we trying to connect with?
2. What do they need to do?
3. What and who are they seeing?
4. What content are they watching?
1. Think about your competitors and the solutions they are currently offering.

2.   What are their opinions?

-     Research what they are saying on social media.

7. Where are they?

8. Where do they hang out?

9. Where can you find them?

10. Who are they?

11. What are their talents, skills?

12. What do they hear?

13. What are they thinking and/or feeling?

Analyze the **Pains and Gains** points that your idea, product or project provides.

Pains:

What worries them about your idea?

Why would they turn your solution down?

Gains:

How can your idea help solve their problems?

How can you convince them that you are the right choice?

Why do a Journey Mapping?

It is often used as an exercise to determine a list of requirements for a project, idea or product, and it will allow you to uncover hidden issues. Doing this exercise would help you and/or your team identify what is bothering the customer and what makes him happy so you can empathize with him.

When to do it?

Journey Maps are created after you've made personas or identified typical users for your project, idea or product.

Who's involved?

All the stakeholders of the project or idea are involved in the *Journey Mapping* to allow valuable conversations to arise through the process of co-authoring the Journey Maps. They *can* also be done solo as an exercise to work through design or product issues.

Time estimate:

1 -2 hours per persona

- Review the persona or typical user's goals for your project, values, and what makes them stressed.

- Have one of the team players assume the role of the persona. The rest of the group should take notes. You can use a mapping application such as BoardThing or Trello.

- Identify what the person's goal is. (Example: my goal is to book a car for my business trip to get around more efficiently).

- Identify what the first step is that they might take in order to accomplish that goal.

- Describe every other possible step in detail that they might take in order to accomplish that goal. (This is a crucial step because it will help you identify where they are heading next).

- Document each step of the scenario. Everyone should provide feedback on the person's journey. (Ask clarifying questions to document the entire scenario).

At the end of this process you should have a good idea if they are willing to pay for your solution.

10. CREATING YOUR MINIMUM VALUE PRODUCT

An **MVP (Minimum Value Product)** is a way to test the market need for your ideas and it helps you validate your assumptions about what features people will crave.

Have you heard about a company called Groupon?

Groupon began as a simple WordPress website, and they began by just offering a coupon to a local Chicago pizza restaurant. The users received their coupons via emails, and the emails had to be sent manually. Their customers liked the content they offered and the type of deals they could access. Once Groupon saw their subscribers grow, they were able to scale up with more features, functions, and the kind of targeted content that their customers wanted.

An industry that does this all the time is television and streaming services when they air their pilots. These pilot episodes test the interest of their potential audiences and the interests of the studios; they are testing their product market fit. The industry uses the feedback to make needed changes, to scrap the pilot completely or to generate new ideas. For example, in "Buffy the Vampire Slayer," their pilot episode' main character was a brunette instead of the popular blonde we got to fall in love with, and the Willow character was played by a different actress.

How can you test your MVP?

1.   Observe, (don't ask) social media response to your ideas.

Are customers willing to pay for your product?

Can you attract potential investors?

2.   Do your research:

Use a keyword research listening site like Answer the Public @ https://bit.ly/3Gpdyxx to find out what kind of question people are asking for around a specific keyword.

11. TIME TO LAUNCH

Now that you have generated your ideas

ORGANIZE THEM

Discover similarities and other ideas that can be combined.

Decide on which ones to **PRIORITIZE** first by starting with the ideas that are easier to implement and the ones that use the least of your resources.

Identify the **PROBLEM THEY SOLVE**.

Map your ideal **CUSTOMER** and what their customer journey would be.

Created your **MVP** (minimum value product/proposition).

Guess what?

It is **TIME TO LAUNCH** them. :)

It is time to tell the whole world about them.

Don't be afraid to share your ideas with other people. We encourage you to share them with lots of people and not just families and friends but with strangers because you would need their honest feedback.

Be humble enough to listen with an open mind.

At every step, you will need to analyze what is working and what is not working.

Make sure to track your progress and milestones.

Launching your ideas is crucial, and we have gathered some suggestions on **HOW TO** launch your ideas.

- Understand that you don't have to implement them all at once.

- It is best to start with the one that you are most comfortable with to start.

- Don't let your nerves get in the way:

Create anticipation for your idea by:

1. Create a Buzz about your launch:

    A. Drop hints on social media.

    B. Tell all those you know.

2. Create a video trailer or audio teaser about them.

    A. Drop hints on social media.

    B. Tell all those you know.

3. Create a video trailer or audio teaser about them.

    A. Videos can be entertaining like movie trailers are.

    B. Videos can be informational like how to use your product.

    C. Videos can bc humorous in a way that showcases your brand personality.

    - Watch these funny commercials in youtube

    - Use an easy-to-use tool to do Creative Marketing like:

Wondershare Videoshop - Free Video Editor.

Unleashing creativity movie

4. Create an audio teaser about them.

    A. Create an audio teaser or podcast.

    B. Use an easy-to-use tool like:

    - Audacity

5. Reach out to influencers and have them promote your product.

    A. Send them a sample of your product for a review.

    B. Pay them to become ambassadors.

    C. Create an affiliated link where they can get paid for a recommendation.

    D. Don't just reach out to big influencers, micro influencers (5k followers or less) are usually more effective.

6. Allow people to Pre-order your product or create a waiting list for it.

    A. Incentivize them with a discount.

    B. Offer an early bird price.

   C. Offer a freebie that they can download.

7. Create a giveaway or competition. Remember that everyone loves a freebie.

   A. Tap into your social media.

   B. Influencer to promote your giveaway and contest.

   C. Create a launch event to produce a buzz.

   D. Your event can be an in-person launch.

   E. Your event can be a virtual launch over zoom or Facebook live.

8. Collaborate with other business owners.

   A. Collaboration would introduce you to a bigger audience.

   B. Collaboration will create favorable connections.

   C. Collaborate with a local artist to create your product packaging.

   D. Collaborate with your local cafe to host the event there.

9. Create a story around your idea and business brand.

   A. This would allow people to connect with your brand in an emotional way.

   B. It will help you stand out from the sea of similar products.

   C. Create a press release to promote your launch.

10. Email campaign

   A. Start collecting emails very early in the launch process and send them notifications about your product.

   B. Have a sign up available on your website, social media, or freebie download.

   C. Keep your email list informed of your progress and

your ideas.

D.   It is always best to write to your list like they were your friends.

E.   Avoid being annoying and sellsy.

F.   Reference those emails that you receive in your own inbox and look forward to reading them to reference and craft your email copywriting style.

G.   Offer your email list the option for early pre-orders.

Whatever option you choose to launch your ideas, the most important thing to remember is to **START**, that is half the battle.

Do not wait for the right time, there is no such thing. The more time you wait to launch, the more time is lost.

How?

Learn to listen to what the market, your customers and stakeholders are saying, even the negative comments (those are the most important because they clearly identify a problem that you need to address).

Even giant companies have to keep changing and innovating or they can risk becoming obsolete.

Do you know of a company called Legos?

In 2003, the beloved brand had accumulated $800M in debt and had run out of cash despite having never reported a loss from 1932 - 1998.

Why?

They had stopped growing as a company and had not added anything new that added value to their offer. That is why they decided to restructure and stop relying on only physical products. Lego innovated by adding digitization and digital products to their physical products by introducing virtual augmented reality (AR) experiences to their business model. This strategy helped them overtake Ferrari in 2015 as the most powerful brand.

Lego's Revival story was published in "Brick by Brick: How LEGO Rewrote the Rules of Innovation and Conquered the Global Toy Industry."

START TAKING ACTION
and remember to
TURN OFF THE DISTRACTIONS.
SET A TIMER and START DOING.
PUSH BACK YOUR OWN RESISTANCE

Be willing to **PIVOT, REFINE** and **SHARPEN** your ideas.

DO NOT BE AFRAID OF CHANGE.
That is the only way to let your ideas grow.

References

6 companies that have successfully Applied Design Thinking: Collective Campus. RSS. (n.d.). Retrieved January 1, 2022, from https://www.collectivecampus.io/blog/6-companies-that-have-successfully-applied-design-thinking

Acumen Academy. (n.d.). Retrieved January 1, 2022, from https://acumenacademy.org/

Alsoasked. AlsoAsked. (n.d.). Retrieved January 1, 2022, from https://www.alsoasked.com/

Amanda. (2017, August 26). *25 crazy inventions that made millions of dollars. #2 is absolutely ridiculous.* LifeBuzz. Retrieved January 1, 2022, from http://www.lifebuzz.com/weird-inventions/5/

The Art of Innovation: Guy kawasaki: Tedxberkeley. YouTube. (2014, February 22). Retrieved March 27, 2022, from https://youtu.be/Mtjatz9r-Vc

Baldauf, K. (2021, October 27). *IBM-Design.* Vimeo. Retrieved January 1, 2022, from https://vimeo.com/370772532

Brainstorming. IDEO U. (n.d.). Retrieved March 3, 2022, from https://www.ideou.com/pages/brainstorming

Brainstorming: How to generate ideas and improve your writing. Brainstorming: How to Generate Ideas for Your Writing | Grammarly Blog. (2021, April 13). Retrieved January 1, 2022, from https://www.grammarly.com/blog/brainstorming/

Burge Hughes Walsh - Six Sigma Specialists. Retrieved January 1, 2022, from https://www.burgehugheswalsh.co.uk/systems-thinking/tools.aspx

Business intelligence for all. SizeUp. (2021, September 24). Retrieved January 1, 2022, from https://company.sizeup.com/

Campaigning for change. Harvard Business Review. (2014, August 1). Retrieved January 1, 2022, from https://hbr.org/2002/07/campaigning-for-change

Courtney, J., About The Author Jonathan Courtney is the UX Director and Founding Partner of AJ&Smart, & Author, A. T. (2016, June 14). *A framework for brainstorming products.* Smashing Magazine. Retrieved January 1, 2022, from https://www.smashingmagazine.com/2016/06/a-framework-for-brainstorming-products/

Craig Stull, P. M. & D. M. S. (2008, July 7). *Tuned in: Uncover the extraordinary opportunities that lead to business breakthroughs.* Apple Books. Retrieved January 1, 2022, from https://books.apple.com/us/audiobook/tuned-in-uncover-the-extraordinary-opportunities-that/id1423819235

Creative thinking: How to increase the dots to connect. YouTube. (2018, June 28). Retrieved March 27, 2022, from https://youtu.be/cYhgIlTy4yY

Dam, R. F., & Siang, T. Y. (n.d.). *Learn how to use the best ideation methods: Scamper.* The Interaction Design Foundation. Retrieved January 1, 2022, from https://www.interaction-design.org/literature/article/learn-how-to-use-the-best-ideation-methods-scamper

Defining growth design: The guide to the role most startups are missing. First Round Review. (n.d.). Retrieved January 1, 2022, from https://review.firstround.com/defining-growth-design-the-guide-to-the-role-most-startups-are-missing

Design thinking 1. Ensemble Video - Publish, Share and Archive Internet Video. (n.d.). Retrieved January 1, 2022, from https://ensemble.syr.edu/hapi/v1/contents/78be5eb4-2387-48ab-82e1-f6f65dc851f5/launch

Design Thinking workshop for Jim Moran Institute's RISE program. Design Minded. (n.d.). Retrieved March 3, 2022, from https://www.designminded.me/jmi

D'Souza , R. (2017, August 19). *Ridiculous ideas that made people ridiculously rich FWD business*. FWD Business. Retrieved March 3, 2022, from https://fwdbusiness.com/2017/08/ideas-that-made-people-rich/

Entrepreneur Consumer Goods Case study examples. Warrior Rising. (n.d.). Retrieved from https://academy.warriorrising.org/wp-content/uploads/2018/12/Entrepreneur-Consumer-Goods-Case-study-examples.pdf

Gatell, D. (2016, August 28). *Identifying customer pain points: The first thing you want to do when determining what to include...* Medium. Retrieved January 1, 2022, from https://medium.com/sozial-monster/identifying-customer-pain-points-the-first-thing-you-want-to-do-when-determining-what-to-include-999fbfeb90df

Global emergency services - aip.org. (n.d.). Retrieved March 3, 2022, from https://www.aip.org/sites/default/files/aipcorp/files/assist-america.pdf

Google. (n.d.). *Share and engage with the design sprint community*. Google. Retrieved January 1, 2022, from https://designsprintkit.withgoogle.com/methodology/phase3-sketch/boot-note-taking

Grant, A. (n.d.). *The surprising habits of original thinkers*. TED. Retrieved January 1, 2022, from https://www.ted.com/talks/adam_grant_the_surprising_habits_of_original_thinkers

Hartman, B. (2022, February 22). *Blog 2*. MDB Communications. Retrieved March 3, 2022, from https://www.mdbcomm.com/news

History and use of brainstorming. History and use of brainstorming including Alex Osborn and Applied Imagination. (n.d.). Retrieved January 1, 2022, from http://www.brainstorming.co.uk/tutorials/historyofbrainstorming.html

How do I get copyright protection for something? Rocket Lawyer. (n.d.). Retrieved January 1, 2022, from https://www.rocketlawyer.com/business-and-contracts/intellectual-property/copyrights/legal-guide/how-to-get-copyright-protection-for-something

How does writing affect your brain? NeuroRelay. (2014, February 15). Retrieved January 1, 2022, from http://neurorelay.com/2013/08/07/how-does-writing-affect-your-brain/

How to protect intellectual property in 5 different ways. Copyrighted.com. (2019, April 18). Retrieved March 3, 2022, from https://www.copyrighted.com/blog/protect-intellectual-property

IDEO design thinking. IDEO. (n.d.). Retrieved March 3, 2022, from https://designthinking.ideo.com/

Ideo U: What is design thinking? YouTube. (2018, December

Niurka Castaneda

5). Retrieved January 1, 2022, from
https://youtu.be/ldYzbV0NDp8

If You can dream it, you can do it. GlobalLinker. (n.d.).
Retrieved January 1, 2022, from
https://www.globallinker.com/mobile/bizforum/article/if-you-can-dream-it-you-can-do-it/17371

Intuitivemind. Free Word Templates. (n.d.). Retrieved March 3,
2022, from
https://www.wordstemplates.org/author/Jake/page/23/

JDN 1-18, Strategy - Joint Chiefs of Staff. (n.d.). Retrieved
January 1, 2022, from
https://www.jcs.mil/portals/36/documents/doctrine/jdn_jg/jdn1_18.pdf?ver=2018-04-25-150439-540

JMI. Design Minded. (n.d.). Retrieved January 1, 2022, from
https://www.designminded.me/jmi

Jon Burgstone and Bill Murphy, J. (2013, July 11). *Why customer pain is your most important resource.* Fast Company.
Retrieved January 1, 2022, from
https://www.fastcompany.com/1844165/why-customer-pain-your-most-important-resource

Jul 01, 2013 B. P. V. E. N. A. (n.d.). *How Lego stopped thinking outside the box and innovated inside the brick.*
Knowledge@Wharton. Retrieved March 3, 2022, from
https://knowledge.wharton.upenn.edu/article/how-lego-stopped-thinking-outside-the-box-and-innovated-inside-the-brick/

Kelley, T., & Littman, J. (2008). *The Ten Faces of Innovation: Ideo's strategies for beating the Devil's advocate and driving creativity throughout your organization.* Profile books.

Making the team: A guide for managers [fifth edition] 9780132968089, 1292060786, 9781292060781, 0132968088.
dokumen.pub. (n.d.). Retrieved March 3, 2022, from

https://dokumen.pub/making-the-team-a-guide-for-managers-fifth-edition-9780132968089-1292060786-9781292060781-0132968088.html

Massoni , K. (n.d.). *BRINGING UP ABABY@: THE BIRTH AND EARLY DEVELOPMENT OF SEVENTEEN MAGAZINE.* kuscholarworks. Retrieved March 3, 2022, from https://kuscholarworks.ku.edu/bitstream/handle/1808/4026/umi-ku-2218_1.pdf

Massoni, K. L. (n.d.). *Kuscholarworks.ku.edu.* Retrieved March 3, 2022, from https://kuscholarworks.ku.edu/bitstream/handle/1808/4026/umi-ku-2218_1.pdf

MCDP 1-2 campaigning - United States Marine Corps. (n.d.). Retrieved January 1, 2022, from https://www.marines.mil/Portals/1/Publications/MCDP%201-2%20Campaigning.pdf

Naskah publikasi - ums. (n.d.). Retrieved March 3, 2022, from http://eprints.ums.ac.id/21158/20/NASKAH_PUBLIKASI.pdf

Navi Radjou: Creative problem-solving in the face of extreme limits. YouTube. (2015, January 12). Retrieved March 27, 2022, from https://youtu.be/cHRZ6OrSvvI

The New York Times. (2019, March 26). *Precrastination: When the early bird gets the shaft.* The New York Times. Retrieved January 1, 2022, from https://www.nytimes.com/2019/03/25/smarter-living/precrastination-when-the-early-bird-gets-the-shaft.html

Open design kit. Journey Mapping. (n.d.). Retrieved January 1, 2022, from http://opendesignkit.org/methods/journey-maps/

Photo Pleine Page. doczz.net. (2017, April 20). Retrieved March 3, 2022, from https://doczz.net/doc/808012/photo-pleine-page

Profit&. (n.d.). *7 real-life examples of successful change management in business*. Enterprise Profit Maximisation. Retrieved January 1, 2022, from https://insights.profitand.com/blog/real-life-examples-of-successful-change-management-in-business

Pun, A. (2021, February 26). *Is there ever a right time to launch your startup idea?: EU-Startups*. EU. Retrieved January 1, 2022, from https://www.eu-startups.com/2021/02/is-there-ever-a-right-time-to-launch-your-startup-idea/

RAHMAWATI, S. O. V. I. A. (n.d.). *Naskah publikasi - ums*. A PRAGMATIC ANALYSIS OF COMMISSIVE UTTERANCES ON TOY STORY MOVIE MANUSCRIPT AND ITS SUBTITLE. Retrieved March 3, 2022, from http://eprints.ums.ac.id/21158/20/NASKAH_PUBLIKASI.pdf

Ranadive, A. (2018, March 19). *Learning from "The ten faces of innovation"*. Medium. Retrieved March 3, 2022, from https://medium.com/@ameet/learning-from-the-ten-faces-of-innovation-4aaf253a9a62

Resources for Online Teaching & Learning: Design. FIU Libraries. (n.d.). Retrieved March 3, 2022, from https://library.fiu.edu/onlineteaching/design

Search listening tool for market, Customer & Content Research. AnswerThePublic. (n.d.). Retrieved January 1, 2022, from https://answerthepublic.com/

Stull, C., Myers, P., & Scott, D. M. (2008). *Tuned in: Uncover the extraordinary opportunities that lead to business breakthroughs*. Amazon. Retrieved March 3, 2022, from The Awl. (2016, May 13). *When we were "seventeen": A history in 47 covers*. Medium. Retrieved January 14, 2022, from https://medium.com/the-awl/when-we-were-seventeen-a-history-in-47-covers-d53f4fa677ee

Tools. IDEO.org. (n.d.). Retrieved January 1, 2022, from

https://www.ideo.org/tools

tuned in: Uncover the extraordinary opportunities that lead to business breakthroughs. Amazon. Retrieved January 1, 2022, from https://www.amazon.com/Tuned-Extraordinary-Opportunities-Business-Breakthroughs/dp/047026036X

Vaughan, P. (2022, February 21). *How to create detailed buyer personas for your business [free persona template]*. HubSpot Blog. Retrieved March 3, 2022, from https://blog.hubspot.com/marketing/buyer-persona-research

Website designed and developed by Zarr - http://www.zarr.com. (n.d.). *System thinking - tools for system thinking*. Burge Hughes Walsh - Six Sigma Specialists. Retrieved January 1, 2022, from https://www.burgehugheswalsh.co.uk/systems-thinking/tools.aspx

What is a work for hire agreement? Rocket Lawyer. (n.d.). Retrieved January 1, 2022, from https://www.rocketlawyer.com/business-and-contracts/employers-and-hr/recruiting-and-hiring/legal-guide/what-is-work-for-hire-agreement

What is an affinity diagram? ASQ. (n.d.). Retrieved January 1, 2022, from https://asq.org/quality-resources/affinity

Where good ideas come from: Steven Johnson. YouTube. (2010, September 21). Retrieved March 27, 2022, from https://youtu.be/0af00UcTO-c

World Leaders in Research-Based User Experience, K. P. (n.d.). *Affinity diagramming: Collaboratively sort UX findings & design ideas*. Nielsen Norman Group. Retrieved March 3, 2022, from https://www.nngroup.com/articles/affinity-diagram/
Write your business plan. (n.d.). Retrieved January 1, 2022, from https://www.sba.gov/business-guide/plan-your-business/write-your-business-plan

The Author

©Christine Marie Sanchez

The author, Niurka Castaneda, is the mother of two incredible kids. She loves to write, travel, and take pictures. Entrepreneurship was a way to find her identity after transitioning from the military and building the brand Amor Umbrella out of a heart shaped, bright red umbrella. She is enthusiastic for veteran entrepreneurial journeys, and under the umbrella of Amor Umbrella, she focuses on education, media, and brand awareness to help inspire, ignite, and educate other veteran entrepreneurs in their own entrepreneurial journey.

Learn more about her @ NiurkaCastaneda.com

Books By the Author

New Business Launch Guide

A Better Business Launch Guide

La Mejor Guía para Comenzar un Negocios

It's all About Time Management

Todo es Cuestión de Manejar tu Tiempo

From Idea to Implementation

La Idea, La Aplicación y La Ejecución

Venture into the Everglades

Aventurarse en el Everglades

The Complete Life Reference Guide

Follow The Author

https://niurkacastaneda.com/

Made in the USA
Columbia, SC
15 July 2022

63348148R00036